Pre-Marital MOT:
A Relationship Inspection

Susan Jane Smith, B.Sc.

Psychotherapist

Published and distributed by:

Counselling in the Forest Publishing
Email: susan@emotionalhealthforemotionalwealth.co.uk
www.emotionalhealthforemotionalwealth.co.uk

The moral right of the author has been asserted.

The author suggests that you seek legal or medical advice for yourself, if appropriate, because this book in no way replaces such advice. This material is supplied for information only and is the subjective opinion of the author. The author and publisher assume no responsibility for your actions in any event.

DEDICATION

To
Rachel Beckett

For her belief in me

For her support

And
For making me
A
Truly
"Gutsy Girl"

Table of Contents

ACKNOWLEDGEMENTS

My thanks to my husband, Richard, for all the hours of proof reading he undertook. Frankie Pothecary of Business Support GL17 has been invaluable with her computer knowledge! Andrew Jamieson of Minuteman Press in Milton Keynes has supported and encouraged and provided technical knowledge where I had none!

Christine Warwick of SHA PR deserves my heartfelt thanks for her support and professional expertise. I also thank Charlotte Hitchings of C-Change for her friendship and faith in me! My thanks goes to Clare Primett of Agincourt Legal. Wendy Guilfoyle, Reflexologist, reduced my stress and increased my creativity and led me to be braver than I thought possible!

Susan Jane Smith, B.Sc.

Reviews of Pre-Marital MOT:
A Relationship Inspection

"Anyone and everyone thinking of getting married or just living with someone should definitely read this book with their partner before taking any decisions. It is a great tool for opening up discussion together on mutual topics you might not ordinarily discuss prior to making decisions based very often on emotions alone. It can pin point areas of different thinking or potential conflict but can also be reassuring when you discover that you and your partner are on the same wavelength about most things." *Carol.*

"Thinking of marriage? Do yourself a favour and read this!

If you're planning to get married, have been in a marriage that failed and want to do better next time, GET THIS BOOK! It might just save you a VERY big mistake!! I personally made a pig's ear of my marriage and several relationships since. I don't intend to make the same mistakes again!! I have to confess more than a passing interest in this book... it was written by my counsellor!

She is a counsellor and psychotherapist with twenty-one years experience in the area of marital counselling. What it does is fill a gaping hole in the self-help and self-improvement market, and also stands alone as what I think should be compulsory reading for anyone intending to tie the knot!

It's divided into short chapters covering all the areas that a couple should consider and discuss, such as Character Traits, Personal Qualities, Spiritual Values (the author doesn't mean religious), Money, Sex, Parenting, Communication Skills. The book is big on TALKING to your partner - in fact the book is pretty useless unless you do! The whole thrust is 'If in any doubt do not get married!', so get talking and sort out the differences. Note 'the differences', not 'any differences'! What the book does is, through quizzes and checklists, highlight all the potential areas of conflict from 'Do you have evidence that your partner is tolerant', through 'Does your partner enjoy their work' to 'Does you partner expect you to put out the rubbish bins'. It puts down in black and white the things that, all too often, destroy marriages... as seen through years of experience in the consulting room.

It is a slim volume, only 86 pages, and widely spaced due to the quizzes and checklists, but I think this is its strength. It's a workbook really, for you and your partner to write in. You could read it through in not much more than an hour and get into the heart of it in less than fifteen minutes. If you want a tome on the subject of marriages and relationships, this is not for you. If you want to give your marriage the best chance of success, buy it. At the very least you will get a different perspective on some of the things that end up destroying relationships. It encourages you to actually complete the quizzes, fill in the agreements in the book and jointly sign them. I am not so sure about signing agreements but, if it's approached in a 'fun but serious' way it can help focus on areas that may otherwise be difficult to talk about. And that, really, is the strength of the book - it focuses the mind on potential problems.

One thing it doesn't do is tell you how to resolve any problems. There are plenty of books out there that have been written to help with those. It's a brief, no-nonsense, summary of what you need, no, MUST, consider before marriage. Unique and brilliant!" *Review by Gerund on Amazon.co.uk.*

"If you are considering tying the knot, this is a must read!" *Rachel B.*

INTRODUCTION

**"Relationships are not problems to be solved
nor contracts to be won.**

They are like plants - to be grown."

Don't live together, conceive children together or set your wedding date until you have talked to each other about the contents of this MOT! In England an MOT is an "inspection". *This is a "relationship inspection".* You really need to be in agreement on all these matters or have found a way to resolve any issues, so that you are truly emotionally committed to the relationship prior to the marriage ceremony. That ceremony is just the beginning of a life together and not an end in itself. Too much emphasis is put on how the ceremony is, rather than on what it means for your life in the future.

If in any doubt do not get married! You don't want to be saying in a few years *"I knew I shouldn't, but I did not want to upset the plans."* Divorce is not only financially costly; it is emotionally much harder to walk away once you are actually married. Start as you mean to go on and do not think you can change your partner - that is how couples end up in counselling years down the line!

People assume that their partner sees life the way they do and so will share their pattern of behaviour, rituals (like Sunday lunch at 1p.m.), and desires (like a holiday at the beach when what you love is an activity packed holiday). The trouble is that each person is thinking like this! You are in danger of running along on your own assumptions and can be miles apart without realising it! Talk. Talk. Talk.

Do you think you can "help" your partner (with debts, lack of self worth, alcoholism, disordered eating or any other issue)? Wrong. Do not try. It is not your job to "fix" their life - it is their responsibility! If you are in this situation the relationship is already unbalanced...not a good place to start. If your prospective partner is unhappy about something, steer them in the direction of a professional to sort it out before you get married. You might also need to look at your own self esteem issues if you are drawn to people who are in some way needy!

CHARACTER TRAITS

Please think about your partner's character. Do you like them as a person? It is not enough to have sexual chemistry between you or for you to like how they look.

If in doubt don't marry. You will not be able to change their character. Do you think that if you love them enough, things will change? You're wrong. Love alone is not enough. You actually need to have inter-personal skills and emotional maturity to make a successful, long-term marriage. Read Judith Waller-stein's book *"The Good Marriage"* (ISBN 0-593-03938-6).

People can change themselves through counselling/ psycho-therapy or will power. They may not want to do so. Do not think that somehow it will be all right. A close relationship like marriage usually highlights difficulties, not solves them. Having children will certainly increase the strains, so do not have a baby to "save" your marriage. It won't, and how would you like it if that was the only reason you were born!

Look at your partner's parents. Are they the kind of people you would choose to spend time with socially? What about siblings and extended family? Do not think that you are just marrying your partner - you are marrying into another family and will need to be able to tolerate them! Notice how your partner's parents relate to each other and the family. If you don't like it, be careful. This is the role model your partner will have grown up with and it will strongly influence your partner's behaviour in your marriage. Just the same is true for you. The lessons you learnt at home will be taken into your marriage unless you talk them through and both actively choose to create new patterns of behaviour.

Have either of you had an affair/cheated in a relationship? Warning! Ask if you don't already know. There may have been good reason for being unhappy in a prior relationship, but having the "insurance policy" of starting another relationship whilst still in an existing one is never a clever move - it can indicate fear of commitment, lack of honesty, lack of respect for the existing partner and worst of all is that it is behaviour likely to be repeated! There can be what Judith Sills Ph.D. calls a "fear of entrapment" so I would strongly suggest you **both** read her book *"A Fine Romance"* (ISBN 0-345-38571-3) to check out her stages of courtship and the psychological stuck points that come up.

When you go through the characteristics you like about your partner make sure you can offer the same in your own character! Opposites may attract, but for the "wrong" reasons. You can be looking for things that your partner can provide for you that you actually need to be developing within yourself.

See the questions over the following pages!

One copy for you and one for your partner!

Questions For You To Answer!

PERSONAL QUALITIES THAT MAKE ALL THE DIFFERENCE!

QUESTIONS FOR
YOU
TO ANSWER!

Do you have evidence (not just a belief) that your partner is:

	Yes	No
Honest	____	____
Trustworthy	____	____
Kind	____	____
Considerate	____	____
Non-judgemental	____	____
Assertive	____	____
Caring	____	____
Fun	____	____
Responsible	____	____
Loyal	____	____
Sexually Attractive	____	____
Patient	____	____
Reliable	____	____
Understanding	____	____
Hardworking (and still able to relax)	____	____
Able to express their thoughts	____	____
Able to express their feelings	____	____
Forgiving and merciful	____	____

Tolerant   _____ _____

Open to Change   _____ _____

Accepting of your feelings   _____ _____

These are the qualities that help people negotiate their differences and their experiences of life.

If your partner has shown signs of being dominant, aggressive, jealous, insecure, lazy, irresponsible (particularly with money) - don't get married. You have a lot to work out FIRST! Wait, and ask them to seek counselling. If they don't - leave. If you are willing to wait and hope and try harder to please you are "loving too much" and you need to seek counselling! Fear of abandonment, misplaced loyalty or low self esteem may be getting in the way of you making a sensible choice.

SWAP YOUR ANSWERS
AND DISCUSS!

If your partner won't bother to answer these questions and is dismissive of this inspection then take it as a warning! Romance is great - a stable personality is what is required for a long term relationship!

PERSONAL QUALITIES THAT MAKE ALL THE DIFFERENCE!

QUESTIONS FOR YOUR PARTNER TO ANSWER!

Do you have evidence (not just a belief) that your partner is:

	Yes	No
Honest	____	____
Trustworthy	____	____
Kind	____	____
Considerate	____	____
Non-judgemental	____	____
Assertive	____	____
Caring	____	____
Fun	____	____
Responsible	____	____
Loyal	____	____
Sexually Attractive	____	____
Patient	____	____
Reliable	____	____
Understanding	____	____
Hardworking (and still able to relax)	____	____
Able to express their thoughts	____	____
Able to express their feelings	____	____

Forgiving and merciful   _____ _____

Tolerant   _____ _____

Open to Change   _____ _____

Accepting of your feelings   _____ _____

These are the qualities that help people negotiate their differences and their experiences of life.

If your partner has shown signs of being dominant, aggressive, jealous, insecure, lazy, irresponsible (particularly with money) - don't get married. You have a lot to work out FIRST! Wait, and ask them to seek counselling. If they don't - leave. If you are willing to wait and hope and try harder to please you are "loving too much" and you need to seek counselling! Fear of abandonment, misplaced loyalty or low self esteem may be getting in the way of you making a sensible choice.

SWAP YOUR ANSWERS
AND DISCUSS!

FUN TEST FOR YOU

Here are some basics for you to think about. What do you expect to happen after you are married? You need to ask each other and talk through the expectations - do not just assume that your partner will meet your expectations!

	Yes	No
Do you think your partner "should" bring you a cup of tea first thing in the morning?	_____	_____
Do you want your partner to bring you breakfast in bed?	_____	_____
Does your partner like more time than you do to get up and get ready in the mornings?	_____	_____
Do you think your partner should be the one to make the bed in the morning?	_____	_____
Does it matter to you if the food dishes are not washed up immediately?	_____	_____
Does your partner like to cook?	_____	_____
Do you think Sunday lunch should be a roast at 1p.m.?	_____	_____
Do you think that Christmas lunch is turkey at 4p.m.?	_____	_____
Does your partner like surprises?	_____	_____

Do you know what your partner likes
to do to relax?   _____ _____

If yes, what? ____
____

Check this out with them please.

Does your partner take sugar in
tea/coffee?   _____ _____

Do you like your partner's favourite
TV programme?   _____ _____

Which is it? ____
____

Does your partner take a bath/shower
daily?   _____ _____

Does your partner put clean clothes on
daily?   _____ _____

Does your partner pick up their
discarded clothes?   _____ _____

Does your partner like to sleep with the
window open?   _____ _____

Does your partner put the top back on
the toothpaste?   _____ _____

Does your partner like the toilet seat lid
to be put down?   _____ _____

Is your partner tidy in their current
home, the way you like?   _____ _____

Do you like some of your partner's
hobbies?   _____ _____

Which ones? ____
____

Do you like some of your partner's   _____ _____
sporting activities?

Which ones? ____
____

Do you share some of the same   _____ _____
interests?

 If yes, which ones
____
____

Do you know your partner's   _____ _____
favourite colour?

What is it? ____
____

Do you like the size and shape of your   _____ _____
partner's body?

Do you know the colour of your   _____ _____
partner's eyes?
*(If not, you have not spent enough time gazing into each other's
eyes during courtship - a worry!)*

Do you know how many children   _____ _____
your partner wants?

Do you know what contraception
your partner wants the two of you   _____ _____
to use?

Do you know where your partner   _____ _____
wants to live now?

Next Year?   _____ _____

Five years time? _____ _____

Ten years time? _____ _____

Does your partner like to have friends _____ _____
around to your marital home?

Do you like your partner's friends? _____ _____
(If not, think long and hard about getting married)

Does your partner like house painting _____ _____
and decorating?

Does your partner have any DIY skills? _____ _____

Would your partner prefer to pay for _____ _____
professional help around the house?

Does your partner expect to do the _____ _____
clothes washing?

Does your partner expect to do _____ _____
the ironing?

Does your partner expect to do the _____ _____
housecleaning?

Does your partner expect to do the _____ _____
gardening?

Does your partner expect to change the _____ _____
spent light bulbs in the house?

Does your partner expect to put out _____ _____
the rubbish bins?

Does your partner expect to clean _____ _____
the car?

Does your partner expect you to take
responsibility for paying the
household bills?   ____ ____

Does your partner want the children to   ____ ____
be in private education?

Does your partner have the ability to   ____ ____
make a budget and stick to the budget?

Have you decided upon the kinds of
decisions that will be taken jointly,   ____ ____
after discussion?

Do you like the same kind of   ____ ____
holiday as your partner?
(Activity/pool/beach/sightseeing)

Does your partner love animals?   ____ ____
*(If you do and your partner is not so keen - choose the pet! Find a
different partner!*
*Your partner won't be happy if they are trying to put up with your
animals.)*

Do you have a pet(s) and can you
agree how they are taken care of   ____ ____
and by whom?

These questions are examples of the little things that can cause
irritation between two people. You will have more than enough
big life issues to deal with and don't need minor ones causing
difficulties! Talk now! Gain clarity between you, please.

Do try to sort these issues out before you get married!

Fill in the Agreement Form!

FUN TEST FOR YOUR PARTNER

Here are some basics for you to think about. What do you expect to happen after you are married? You need to ask each other and talk through the expectations - do not just assume that your partner will meet your expectations!

	Yes	No
Do you think your partner "should" bring you a cup of tea first thing in the morning?	____	____
Do you want your partner to bring you breakfast in bed?	____	____
Does your partner like more time than you do to get up and get ready in the mornings?	____	____
Do you think your partner should be the one to make the bed in the morning?	____	____
Does it matter to you if the food dishes are not washed up immediately?	____	____
Does your partner like to cook?	____	____
Do you think Sunday lunch should be a roast at 1p.m.?	____	____
Do you think that Christmas lunch is turkey at 4p.m.?	____	____

Does your partner like surprises?   _____ _____

Do you know what your partner likes   _____ _____
to do to relax?

If yes, what? ____
____

Check this out with them please.

Does your partner take sugar in   _____ _____
tea/coffee?

Do you like your partner's favourite   _____ _____
TV programme?

Which is it? ____
____

Does your partner take a bath/shower   _____ _____
daily?

Does your partner put clean clothes on   _____ _____
daily?

Does your partner pick up their   _____ _____
discarded clothes?

Does your partner like to sleep with the   _____ _____
window open?

Does your partner put the top back on   _____ _____
the toothpaste?

Does your partner like the toilet seat lid _____ _____
to be put down?

Is your partner tidy in their current   _____ _____
home, the way you like?

Do you like some of your partner's hobbies?   ____ ____

Which ones? ____

____

Do you like some of your partner's sporting activities?   ____ ____

Which ones? ____

____

Do you share some of the same interests?   ____ ____

If yes, which ones? ____

____

Do you know your partner's favourite colour?   ____ ____

What is it? ____

____

Do you like the size and shape of your partner's body?   ____ ____

Do you know the colour of your partner's eyes?   ____ ____
(If not, you have not spent enough time gazing into each other's eyes during courtship - a worry!)

Do you know how many children your partner wants?   ____ ____

Do you know what contraception your partner wants the two of you to use?   ____ ____

Do you know where your partner wants to live now?   ____ ____

Next Year?   ____ ____

Five years time? ____ ____

Ten years time? ____ ____

Does your partner like to have friends ____ ____
around to your marital home?

Do you like your partner's friends? ____ ____
(If not, think long and hard about getting married)

Does your partner like house painting ____ ____
and decorating?

Does your partner have any DIY skills? ____ ____

Would your partner prefer to pay for ____ ____
professional help around the house?

Does your partner expect to do the ____ ____
clothes washing?

Does your partner expect to do ____ ____
the ironing?

Does your partner expect to do the ____ ____
housecleaning?

Does your partner expect to do the ____ ____
gardening?

Does your partner expect to change the ____ ____
spent light bulbs in the house?

Does your partner expect to put out ____ ____
the rubbish bins?

Does your partner expect to clean
the car?   _____ _____

Does your partner expect you to take
responsibility for paying the
household bills?   _____ _____

Does your partner want the children to   _____ _____
be in private education?

Does your partner have the ability to   _____ _____
make a budget and stick to the budget?

Have you decided upon the kinds of
decisions that will be taken jointly,   _____ _____
after discussion?

Do you like the same kind of holiday
as your partner?   _____ _____
(Activity/pool/beach/sightseeing)

Does your partner love animals?   _____ _____
*(If you do and your partner is not so keen - choose the pet! Find a
different partner!*
*Your partner won't be happy if they are trying to put up with your
animals.)*

Do you have a pet(s) and can you agree how they are taken care
of   _____ _____
and by whom?

These questions are examples of the little things that can cause
irritation between two people. You will have more than enough
big life issues to deal with and don't need minor ones causing
difficulties! Talk now! Gain clarity between you, please.

Do try to sort these issues out before you get married!

Fill in the Agreement Form!

OUR AGREEMENT!

This is an opportunity for you to agree and record your discussions - you can always renegotiate!

The reason for writing this information down is so that no one forgets!

OUR AGREEMENT!

We agree that **we want/don't want** a cup of tea first thing in the morning.

We agree that breakfast in bed is _____________

We agree that the bed will be made by _____ when _____

Dishes will be washed up by _____ when _____

The cooking will be done by _____ when _____

Meals will be _____________

Celebratory meals will be _____________

We agree that surprises are _____________

We agree that it is ok to relax by _____________

The TV remote control will be kept where? _____

Baths/showers will be taken _____________

Clean clothes will be put on how frequently? _____

_____ will be responsible for picking up discarded clothes.

The bedroom window **will be open/not open** at night.

Toothpaste tops **will/will not be** put back on.

The toilet lid **will/will not be** put down after use.

Tidiness is the responsibility of _____________

Hobbies will/will not be carried out in the house.

_____ amount of time is to be dedicated to sporting activities.

Contraception is the responsibility of ___________

We have agreed that we will start out living ___________

We will live ___________ next year.

We will live ___________ in five years time.

We plan to live ___________ in ten years time.

We agree that friends come to our home by **dropping in/invitation/by prior mutual agreement.**

The maintenance and decor of the home is the responsibility of ___________

The clothes washing is the responsibility of ___________

The ironing is the responsibility of ___________

The house cleaning is the responsibility of ___________

Any garden maintenance is the responsibility of ___________

Light bulb replacement is the responsibility of ___________

Rubbish bins will be put out by ___________

Any car cleaning will by the responsibility of ___________

Pets will be the responsibility of ___________

Household bills will be paid by ___________

Decisions will be taken jointly regarding ___________

Holidays will be arranged by ___________

Signed: ___________   **Signed:** ___________

Dated: ___________

SPIRITUAL VALUES

Please talk all this through and don't assume your partner will share your thoughts:

- How important is it to you to be married in a religious ceremony?

- Have you said what you believe in to your partner?

- Which religion and what that means to you?

- Which church (or equivalent) and how often do you want to attend?

- Would you want your partner to come with you?

- Would you want your children to be brought up with your beliefs?

- If there was some unforeseen accident or illness would you want palliative care only?

- If you were to die unexpectedly, would you want your organs donated?

- If you didn't have time to make arrangements together, do you know where your partner would want to be buried? Or if they want to be cremated?

Don't get married until you have resolved any conflicts in this section!

MONEY
FOR YOU TO ANSWER!

This can be one of the most difficult areas in a marriage if you are not in agreement about how to handle your financial matters. It will really help your marital future if you talk ahead of time. The person who controls the money controls a lot of power and influence within the relationship and it is important that this control is shared equally if at all possible.

Think about these questions and discuss together each other's perceptions:

- Is your partner ambitious?

- Will that ambition affect you regarding how often you move areas to pursue their career goals?

- Does your partner enjoy their work? *(This is significant as their unhappiness could affect their home life and they might want to change jobs/careers. This could impact on the marriage.)*

- What would you do if one of you is made redundant?

- Would it be ok if one of you wanted to change jobs?

- What percentage of their income would your partner choose to save each month?

- Do you know the amount of money that your partner earns?

POST MARITAL BUDGET

Now is the time to draft a budget so you can look at how you will live in the future!

MONEY FOR YOUR PARTNER TO ANSWER!

This can be one of the most difficult areas in a marriage if you are not in agreement about how to handle your financial matters. It will really help your marital future if you talk ahead of time. The person who controls the money controls a lot of power and influence within the relationship and it is important that this control is shared equally if at all possible.

Think about these questions and discuss together each other's perceptions:

- Is your partner ambitious?

- Will that ambition affect you regarding how often you move areas to pursue their career goals?

- Does your partner enjoy their work? (This is significant as their unhappiness could affect their home life and they might want to change jobs/careers. This could impact on the marriage.)

- What would you do if one of you is made redundant?

- Would it be ok if one of you wanted to change jobs?

- What percentage of their income would your partner choose to save each month?

- Do you know the amount of money that your partner earns?

POST MARITAL BUDGET

Now is the time to draft a budget so you can look at how you will live in the future!

MONEY DOES MATTER
YOU REALLY CANNOT LIVE ON LOVE!

OUR AGREEMENT!

The lifestyle we want is

____

____

Our policy is that there is a joint account to cover all expenditures/household expenses only/other

Our policy on one person spending out of the joint account is that **it's OK no matter what amount/It is to be discussed and agreed ahead of time.**

If one person spends without agreement they will compensate the other by:

____

Our policy **is/is not** that we will each retain _______ % of income in individual accounts for individual use.

We will create a budget and it will be managed by _______

There will be a **weekly/monthly/quarterly/yearly** review of our budget.

Our policy is to save _______ % for the purpose of

Signed: _______________   Signed: _______________

Dated: _______________

SEX

Before beginning a sexual relationship please try to foster honesty, trust, emotional closeness, mutual respect and communication skills. If these are not already in place don't have sex and certainly don't get into the legal commitment of marriage. If you strengthen the relationship first it will enhance the sexual connection and experience so that you can delight in the giving and receiving of physical pleasure and satisfaction. When people feel emotionally secure they are more likely to experience foreplay and orgasm in a more satisfying manner.

Do you understand how your body works so that you can tell your partner what you like and what you don't enjoy? Masturbate if not and find out! Read *"The Joy of Sex"* Edited by Alex Comfort, M.B., Ph.D. as a fundamental manual and *"The Relate Guide to Sex in a Loving Relationship"* by Sarah Litvinoff to ensure you know all you need to know.

Sex may be considered to be for the procreation of children. It is important to have fun along the way! Do try before you buy! I am not a proponent of children being born out of wedlock. Neither am I keen on people not having sex before marriage...I think of a couple who came to me eighteen years after getting married who were unhappy about their sex life - they did not know that a major part of their distress was that they had not realised the man had premature ejaculation problems and was not able to satisfy his wife with penetrative sex. They didn't talk about it and therefore could not get it fixed and had both been miserable for years without need. This problem could have been identified and options sought if they had sex before marriage!

Have you talked through whether you have the same levels of desire for affection - holding hands, hugging, kissing and is it all right with both of you if you show affection in public? If not, sort it out as this will cause constant friction between you that undermines a marriage.

Have either of you had a "bad" sexual experience previously? Forced sexual contact, or any other sexualised memories that might create flashbacks and interfere with pleasurable sex now? If so, go to counselling before marriage.

Sex is great - keep it that way - have fun!

PARENTING

Children tend to be parented as you remember your parents doing it and that is fine if your childhood was joyous and positive. Your partner may have had a similar experience, but on the other hand your partner may have had a different style of parenting experience and be influenced by that parental style.

Please talk before conception and it really does make a child feel more secure if that conception comes within the legal framework of a marriage, so do think about that first. There are legal benefits to being married before having children...get legal advice if you need it.

Do you want children?
Does your partner want children?
Have you actually asked your partner?

IT IS CRITICAL THAT YOU DON'T JUST ASSUME THEY WANT WHAT YOU WANT!

Do you want to plan parenthood?
When do you want children?
How many children?
How many months or years apart?

THIS ALL NEEDS CAREFUL DISCUSSION BEFORE MARRIAGE!

A Parenting Plan was originally created as part of separation/divorce procedures. It is an effective tool for parents to use to consider the needs of their children. I am including some questions for the two of you to discuss, so that you think about these issues before you even conceive the children! A bit old fashioned perhaps! I do realise that many of you will be inheriting children from previous relationships!

This is about how you intend to parent together - whether you stay together for life or separate at a later date the needs of the children need to be paramount!

If you are living together or marrying when there are already children some of these questions may be more urgent than oth-erwise! This is really just to get you talking and sharing your ideas!

Questions to be answered by *you:*

1. Who do you consider to be "the family"?

- You and your partner?

- Children from a previous relationship?

- Your biological parents?

- The parents who raised you *(not always the same as the ones who gave birth)* i.e. the "grandparents"?

- Your aunts and uncles?

- Your cousins?

- Any other significant people related to you?

2. What surnames will be used by the children?
(in reformed families there might be several options)

3. What provisions need to be made for child care if neither of you are available? *(Grandparents, aunts, etc.).* Do those people have the ability to contact you if there was a medical emergency?

4. If you are both working outside of the home, who will be the person responsible for the childcare (like food, supervision of baths/clothes, etc)?
Nanny? Au Pair? Relative? One of you will give up work?

5. Who will look after the child(ren) if they are not well?

6. What inoculations do you agree can be given to your child? MMR?

7. Do you both agree with blood transfusions being given to your child?

8. What dental care do you think is required? Teeth to be brushed once/twice a day or after every meal?

9. What sex education do you want provided to your child?

- At what age?

- Who is to do that? Which one of you? The school only?

10. When is the "right" time from your point of view for children to know about:

- Contraception?

- Drugs?

- Alcohol?

- Cigarettes?

- Gambling (including scratch cards)?

- Solvent Abuse?

- Stealing/Lying?

- Truancy?

- Healthy Eating? *(instead of anorexia/bulimia/comfort eating)*

11. What agreed policy do you have for each of the above?

12. Will one or both of you attend the school parents evenings/school plays/sports events?

13. Who will oversee the children's homework, to make sure it's done or to provide help?

14. How will you fund special school trips?

15. Will your children be allowed to bring their friends home?

16. Where will your children be allowed to go to play? Friends homes, playground, etc.

17. Do you know how to contact your children's friend's parents?

18. Are there religious or cultural issues to discuss?

Questions to be answered by *your partner*:

1. Who do you consider to be "the family"?

    - You and your partner?

    - Children from a previous relationship?

    - Your biological parents?

    - The parents who raised you *(not always the same as the ones who gave birth)* i.e. the "grandparents"?

    - Your aunts and uncles?

    - Your cousins?

    - Any other significant people related to you?

2. What surnames will be used by the children? *(in reformed families there might be several options)*

3. What provisions need to be made for child care if neither of you are available? *(Grandparents, aunts, etc.).* Do those people have the ability to contact you if there was a medical emergency?

4. If you are both working outside of the home, who will be the person responsible for the childcare (like food, supervision of baths/clothes, etc)?

5. Nanny? Au Pair? Relative? One of you will give up work?

6. Who will look after the child(ren) if they are not well?

7. What inoculations do you agree can be given to your child? MMR?

8. Do you both agree with blood transfusions being given to your child?

9. What dental care do you think is required? Teeth to be brushed once/twice a day or after every meal?

10. What sex education do you want provided to your child?

    - At what age?

    - Who is to do that? Which one of you? The school only?

- When is the "right" time from your point of view for children to know about:

- Contraception?

- Drugs?

- Alcohol?

- Cigarettes?

- Gambling (including scratch cards)?

- Solvent Abuse?

- Stealing/Lying?

- Truancy?

- Healthy Eating? (instead of anorexia/bulimia/comfort eating)

11. What agreed policy do you have for each of the above?

12. Will one or both of you attend the school parents evenings/ school plays/ sports events?

13. Who will oversee the children's homework, to make sure it's done or to provide help?

14. How will you fund special school trips?

15. Will your children be allowed to bring their friends home?

16. Where will your children be allowed to go to play? Friends homes, playground, etc.

17. Do you know how to contact your children's friend's parents?

18. Are there religious or cultural issues to discuss?

OUR AGREEMENT!

We agree that *"the family"* is made up of:

____

(list the names of the people so everyone is clear about who is in and who is not)

We agree that the family surname to be used is
(and list others if more than one option affects different children)

We agree that _______________ will take prime responsibility for childcare.

We agree that our policy is:

Contraception: _______________________________

  Drugs: _______________________________

  Alcohol: _____________________________

  Cigarettes: __________________________

  Gambling: ____________________________

  Solvent Abuse: _______________________

  Stealing/Lying: ______________________

  Truancy _____________________________

  Healthy Eating: ______________________

The other matters we agree upon are:

____

____

Signed: _____________________ Signed: _____________________

Dated: _____________________

NB If you do end up divorcing in the future, please check out the comprehensive Children's Questionnaire on my website: www.emotionalhealthforemotionalwealth.co.uk.

This was created by me originally and developed with Neil Robinson (solicitor, judge and mediator) for the Family Mediators Association.

Please also talk about my "Alternatives to Smacking Your Child" as you do need to be in agreement about the issue of discipline. Would your partner agree that:

When life gets on top of you and you feel like lashing out?

STOP!

Would you and your partner agree to:

- Take 3 slow deep breaths.

- Then take 10! Breathe out slowly.

- Let your brain slow down.

- Think before acting.

- Step back from the situation.

Would you and your partner be able to think?

- Will hitting actually work?

- Will hitting just instil fear and resentment?

- What am I actually trying to achieve?

If you or your partner were still angry, would you find an alternative to create calm?

- Phone a friend or relative.

- Sit down.

- Write down thoughts and feelings.

- Hug a pillow or cushion.

When it feels like your child is not doing what you want it can be counterproductive to just lash out. Whilst the subject of discipline has been controversial lately I would still suggest that if looked at from the point of view of the child, Mum or Dad hitting out just looks confusing. There is usually a scary facial expression that goes with the smack and that conveys not just displeasure but usually hatred - far too strong a response for any childhood situation. If this is you it is probably because you feel stressed, tired, and angry about other things or simply out of control.

Hitting your child won't fix any of those issues.

Can you and your partner: learn to be assertive, learn to manage your stress, and learn to manage your anger.

These are responsible parenting skills.

At a quiet time when you feel relaxed and ok come up with some "house rules", write them down and put them up where everyone can see. Make these appropriate to the age of your children. Then everyone knows what is expected. Also, come up with some "consequences" for breaking those rules that are in proportion to the "crime" of the child and deprive them of a "privilege" like TV or going out or removal of a toy for a brief period of time. Always keep your word. Consistency and boundaries are what make children feel safe. Yes, they will kick (sometimes literally) against these limits. Just stick to what you have said. "No" does have to mean "no" so think before you say it and make sure that you can stand by what you have said. Inconsistency creates confusion for anyone, at any age.

If you think you were wrong, apologise to your child. That is demonstrating respect. Children thrive on being treated with respect and dignity. If you were not treated that way in your childhood you may not know how to do that, so find somewhere to learn it (counselling can help).

Punishment is not the same as a consequence. You are preparing the child for adult life. The bank manager gives you a consequence for being overdrawn in the way of a fee; you don't go straight to prison. Are you sure that your punishments fit the "crime"? Have you stopped to think about the message that you are giving your child?

Discipline is necessary. It is about teaching what is acceptable behaviour, so you need to actually say what would have been the preferred behaviour in the situation - children cannot guess and should not be expected to "know" what you think.

Speak to them respectfully. This is how you teach them to speak to you. Fundamentally, you will get back what you teach, so if you don't like your child's behaviour, look at your own.

Many children are bored at home because parents do not interact with them. Find interesting and fun activities to stimulate the child's mind. Simply collecting them from school and leaving them to their own devices is not parenting them…it is not enough to feed them and provide a roof over their heads. They need your time and attention. Yes, you may be tired. You are still a parent and that implies responsibilities whether you like it or not. Think about this before you conceive your next child!

Always remember to tell your children that you love them. Children do need to actually hear the words. The words convey acceptance. The child's behaviour may not always be acceptable and when you speak to them you need to point out that it is the behaviour, not the person, that you dislike. When you say "bad girl" or "bad boy" you are fundamentally damaging the child's self worth. Ultimately, what will they have to lose by continuing to be "bad"? Any attention is better than no attention, so why not just go on acting out? This is not good parenting. If that happened to you, go to counselling instead!

Years ago I heard a father say to a crying toddler "If you keep on crying I'll give you something to cry about" that just brought on more tears. It might have stopped the child, but if it had, it would have stopped the tears for all the wrong reasons. He was trying to gain control through terror. It won't work in the long term. It looks like a quick "fix", but not really. It accomplishes nothing. A cuddle would have worked better if he really wanted to stop the tears.

Now you may be wondering "Who is she to be telling me how to raise my children?" Well, my comments are subjective and my personal opinion - they come from listening to hundreds of adults over the last twenty years talking about their childhoods. Can you and your partner agree:

Your child is an investment.

Spend quality time with them and the investment will repay you.

COMMUNICATION SKILLS

Communication is about talking in a direct, honest way and actually listening without interrupting - speaking when the other person has finished. Not being distracted by what you want to say back!

It is not always easy to "really" listen. Many people listen with only part of their attention actually on what is being said. They can be thinking about other things, including what they want to say. Sometimes you may not like what is being said so you "block" out the words by humming, whistling, singing to yourself, etc. None of this will actually make what is being communicated go away. You will be better served if you face what is being said.

Active listening requires using both your ears and your eyes! You can notice the other person's "body language" and that will help you to understand what is being said. Sometimes the body language will reinforce the words...at other times it may contradict what is being expressed. If there is contradiction consider giving more credibility to the behaviour than the words! Body language is non-verbal communication. You can enhance your own communication by using it effectively.

- When direct communication is taking place, two people face each other "squarely"...with the distance between them that feels appropriate to them both.

- Folded arms and turning your body away is "closed" and to be avoided if you want to be effective.

- When listening intently lean forward slightly or tilt your head to one side - it aids your concentration and conveys your interest

- Make eye contact and maintain it if possible.

- Relax your shoulders down - holding tension will not assist you in what you want to convey.

- Look as if you are listening (not looking out the window, at the TV, newspaper etc.)

- Ask questions.

- Stay focused on one topic at a time.

- Test out with the other person what they believe they have heard you say (intention as well as actual words). Get them to reflect what you have said back to you, to check that you have truly been understood BEFORE you go on to say anything else. That is best done if you both practise this when there is a serious topic - not necessarily when the material is light hearted.

- Try not to have preconceived ideas about what you think the other person wants to say...don't jump to conclusions...don't make assumptions. This just gets in the way and may or may not have anything to do with the other person's reality!

- Evaluate what you have heard and reflect it back to the person speaking to ensure that you have actually understood.

- Be aware of your own reactions - how you are feeling.

- Are there any unspoken messages? If you think so, ask. Check it out.

- Notice how something is said, not just what is said.

- Think about the future and what the issue is rather than your position on the issue.

- Speaking in terms of "how" and "what" or asking the other person "how" or "what" questions is more effective than asking or saying "why". "Why" produces defensiveness on the part of people and is not as effective as you are more likely to end up arguing rather than resolving an issue.

- Say what would improve the circumstances for you.

- Think about how the situation is a problem for you and explain that to the other person. This is a better approach than just saying what you want.

- Ask what the other person would do to create a different situation, if they could "wind the clock back."

- Ask what the other person would like as an ideal situation - if you both do this you might find some mutual understanding and can move towards the ideal.

- Do you know what "triggers" an argument between you? Discuss the trigger and you may find that the heat is taken out of the disagreement.

- Ask for a specific change in behaviour rather than just saying that something is not alright.

- Ask yourself if you really do want to resolve the conflict or do you like arguing? Are you actually interested in creating solutions? What is the alternative to reaching an agreement?

- Ask yourself how the situation would look if you were the other person - try to get some insight into their point of view!

- What is the smallest thing you would be prepared to do to meet the other person's needs? What would they be willing to do...ask.

- Focus on the future and what could be done differently in the future (instead of blaming anyone for the past).

- In a disagreement state facts. State feelings separately!

At other times, you keep people at "arm's length" if you only speak about trivial matters like the weather or if you just stick to the facts. You are not disclosing your personal thoughts and feelings (hopes, dreams, desires, fears, dislikes, disappointments) and they are what will allow people to really get to know you. Dropping your barriers and sharing these builds relationships. Relationships don't get formed and they don't last unless you can be direct in also saying what you don't like or don't want.

Couples have to learn that to disagree is normal and you need to accept that you may each see the world differently. Slight differences are normal - lots of huge ones probably indicate you are with the wrong person!

If you can laugh together you are off to a flying start. It is the counterpoint for being able to be cross with each other, and you will get cross! The secret is to learn to negotiate (win/win) instead of compromise (lose/lose) and instead of trying to get your own way (win/lose).

- Can you identify what the most frequent disagreement is about between you? What do you each do when you disagree? Speak directly, withdraw, shout, sulk, and hit out?

- Are you willing to make allowances for your partner if they are tired, stressed, unwell, and overly anxious? Do you say sorry and forgive each other for the hurt caused even if you cannot agree about the viewpoint?

Think before you speak.

DOMESTIC ABUSE
AND
SOME TIPS FOR HANDLING AGGRESSION!

The classic situation is male to female violence so that is the way this section is written. I have certainly worked with people where it has been the other way around. Gay and lesbian relationships can also be violent. Emotional abuse can be as damaging as actual violence or the threat of violence. What values do you and your partner share around being in a non-abusive relationship?

Some men still want a "traditional" wife who cooks and cleans and takes care of the children and allows him to be the "boss". For some men this also means control of wife, children, money and life! In the classic situation, there are some issues that have traditionally put a woman at greater risk: wanting to be independent/"liberated", if the man is less educated or earning less money than the woman. Differences in religion or ethnicity can also put a strain on some marriages. Please make sure that you know what you each expect from the marriage. Talk lots!

Certainly do not marry or live together or have children together if there is already a history of violence between you. If either of you has been in an abusive relationship before go to counselling NOW.

Ask your partner about their behaviour in previous relationships. Be brave. Ask directly if they have ever hit, kicked, punched, bitten or stalked anyone. Ask if they have ever used a weapon to hurt another person or animal - even if this was a man in a pub fight you need to see it as a warning and think carefully before continuing. It indicates a willingness to breach a certain boundary about physical violence and once that has been breached it is easier for it to happen again, in my opinion.

You do have the right to know if you are about to commit your life to this person. You do also have a need to know. If the answer is "yes" to any of this don't ignore it - you need to know what psychological changes your partner has made in therapy if any of this behaviour has already occurred in their handling of life. DO NOT accept a comment that it was the other person "who made me do it". That is rubbish! Technically we are each responsible for our own behaviour and the choices we make. There really is no such thing as "I couldn't help myself."

If either of you has been violent in a past relationship do not get married…run!

If you really want to be together couples counselling and anger management needs to take place before you think about living together, getting married or having children!

It's too great a risk.

Too many people ignore warning signs about being in a dangerous relationship!

Here are some questions to think about:

- Is your man insecure?

- Does he expect/want you to nurture him?

- Does he get jealous?

- Is he charming/manipulative (does everyone think he's lovely, but behind closed doors he is not as nice to you)?

- Is he unable/unwilling to say "sorry"?

- Have either of you used "street drugs"?

- Are either of you workaholics?

- Are either of you addicted to gambling, shopping to excess, or eating disordered (anorexic, bulimic or obese)?

A pre-cursor to a violent marriage is, sometimes, violence in the childhood home. *Ask:*

- Did Mum and Dad hit each other?

- Did Mum and Dad shout at each other?

- Did they hit you or a sibling?

- Were they violent to a pet?

- Did anyone punch the door or wall, etc.?

- Was over-consumption of alcohol or drug use a problem for anyone in your family of origin?

The ultimate goal needs to be to resolve conflict.

Without violence or abuse!

The initial objective when there is conflict that is non-violent is to handle the situation without being drawn into a heated argument as that will not resolve anything - people just shouting at each other does not work. Neither does it work if someone is trying to intimidate the other (punching walls, threats of violence "I'll slap you if you don't stop…", or hitting a person, child or pet).

If you are the person feeling angry:

- Ask yourself what you are hurt about - under anger there is an emotional pain of some sort. If you can say what the pain is the people around you may respond differently than when you express yourself angrily.

- Take three slow deep breaths before speaking.

- Write down your feelings to take the "heat" out of them or say the feeling to an empty chair to practice getting your feelings "off your chest" in a safe way.

- Speak to the person/child with whom you are in conflict - start by using their first name and asking them if they are willing to listen to what you have to say. There is no point in saying it if they are reading the newspaper, watching TV, not interested, etc.

- Talk "with" them not "at" them…this is about choosing the words you say - not just "nagging".

- If they are not willing to listen, you may have to look for another way of dealing with the situation or ask for a time to be identified when they would be willing to listen, e.g. when that TV programme is finished.

- Change how or what you would usually say or do in this

situation - it tends to get people's attention.

If someone else is angry with you do not react - take your time and act. Be calm and firm. Be assertive not passive or aggressive:

- Decide if you are truly willing to hear what they have to say.

- Let the other person know that you understand that they are upset.

- Ask for **specific** information so that you can both identify what the cause of the discontent is about…e.g. "Can you tell me a little more about how you believe this situation has occurred?".

- Stay still and quiet and listen respectfully…not butting in to defend yourself…wait until they have vented the anger.

- Let the other person know what the impact of their aggression is on you…e.g. "The message I get is that you think…".

- Be honest - agree or disagree.

- If you disagree you too need the other person's willingness to listen.

- Ignore aggressive and offensive comments - usually put in to get you engaged in an aggressive way and then not really resolve anything…just return to the status quo…recurring arguments.

- Increase the other person's awareness of the impact they are having by asking "Do you know that when you shout so loudly, it is hard to take in what you are actually saying?" "I find the tone of your voice offensive; please stop talking to me like a child in this way."

- When they shout, you speak softly.

- Sort out "facts" from assumptions or interpretations.

- Ignore putdowns - they are a signal that the person is having difficulty coping - don't take them personally and then escalate the aggression by reacting.

- Keep focused on the issue at hand - don't bring in other things you are cross about.

- Re-focus by stating what needs to happen about the original unsatisfactory situation.

- Find something to do about it - apologise (and ask for your apology to be accepted), put right what the other person says is wrong - change behaviour or agree that you will have to disagree with each other.

- Teach this information to the people with whom you are usually in conflict. Take responsibility for your own behaviour. If there are verbal put-downs get counselling now. Remember no adult, child (or pet) deserves to be hit... hitting is using domination to get an outcome - it creates fear not a true resolution of the situation.

If there is physical violence - leave the relationship.

DO NOT MARRY!

ABOUT THE AUTHOR

Susan Jane Smith was a psychotherapist in private practice from 1987 until 2009. She was born in New Hampshire, U.S.A. and because of her English mother, Sue grew up in Lydney, Gloucestershire, England. She has returned to this area and lives with the tranquillity provided by The Royal Forest of Dean.

Previously Sue had a successful counselling practice in Milton Keynes, Buckinghamshire, England for 17 years. Her professional education comes mainly from the U.S.A. where she was studying for her masters degree in community psychology when her father died and she returned to England with her mother.

Sue was a divorce mediator for five years with the Family Mediators Association and she was also a professional practice consultant for the U.K. College of Family Mediation. She brings to this publication that experience as she would like people to stop and think about their relationships. Sue would also like people to be empowered to create an emotionally wealthy world!

Other books by the same author:

'Emotional Health for Emotional Wealth'

The View from a Therapist's Office

ISBN 978-0-9553698-3-4

£6.99 $9.99 €8.69

Publisher: *Counselling in the Forest Publishing*

Child abuse, bullying, rape, domestic violence, alcoholism and depression are forms of emotional pain that need to be healed before a person can have emotional health.

The subtitle of this book is *'The View from a Therapist's Office'* because the author was a Psychotherapist for over 20 years who dealt with these traumas. Susan Jane Smith B.Sc. was also a Professional Practice Consultant for the U.K.College of Family Mediation.

There are also chapters on love, parenting through divorce, anxiety, stress and bereavement. Her experience led her to identify the changes people can make to move themselves from pain to health and on to emotional wealth. That wealth not only creates happier people and healthier finances - it increases people's integrity, compassion, respect and serenity which is something the author believes the world needs!

www.EmotionalHealthforEmotionalWealth.co.uk

"Harry Is Home! A Cat Compendium"

ISBN 978-0-9553698-1-0

Publisher: *Counselling in the Forest Publishing*

"Harry looks like an angel when asleep." He's a rescue cat enjoying a better life now and who inspired this book of true cat tales. Tears and laughter!